OPPORTUNITIES EDITION

BOLD
Questions

52 questions
to shape how you
take advantage of
your opportunities

Jill J. Johnson, MBA

Johnson
Consulting
Services
Marketing & Management Consultants

Other books by Jill J. Johnson:

From the BOLD Questions Series

BOLD Questions – Business Strategy Edition
BOLD Questions – Leadership Edition
BOLD Questions – Decision Making Edition

Learn more about Jill online and check out her
free white papers at:
www.jcs-usa.com

OPPORTUNITIES EDITION

BOLD
Questions

52 questions
to shape how you
take advantage of
your opportunities

Jill J. Johnson, MBA

Johnson
Consulting
Services
Marketing & Management Consultants

BOLD Questions – Opportunities Edition

Copyright © 2017 Jill J. Johnson

Published by Johnson Consulting Services
Minneapolis, Minnesota
www.jcs-usa.com

Book Design by Chris Mendoza

For information on Jill or on how to order bulk copies of this book,
or the BOLD Questions series, contact her at:
www.jcs-usa.com

ISBN: 978-0-9984236-1-6

Printed in the United States of America

This book is dedicated to my clients.

You have inspired me and taught me so much about how to develop impactful strategies, take advantage of opportunities, lead effectively and make difficult decisions.

ABOUT JILL

An award-winning management consultant, Jill J. Johnson has personally impacted $4 billion worth of business decisions through her consulting work. She is in the board rooms, the back rooms and the executive suites where complex decisions are being made, impacting the future of clients located throughout the United States, as well as in Europe and Asia. She knows what it takes to develop and implement strategies for turnarounds or growth that get results.

Jill is a widely-respected business executive and leader who has been a member of the boards of directors and executive committees of a variety of business, professional and governmental boards. She has served on two federal boards under three different United States presidents representing both political parties.

Jill has won numerous honors for her business acumen, her leadership savvy, mentorship skills and her entrepreneurial successes. Jill is also one of the first women ever inducted into both the Minnesota Women Business Owners Hall of Fame and the Top Women in Finance Hall of Fame.

Over the years, Jill has been quoted on a range of management issues in national publications including *The Wall Street Journal, The New York Times, Inc., Money Magazine* and *Entrepreneur*. She has appeared as a thought leader on a variety of radio and television programs for business. She is a 4th generation entrepreneur who grew up in a family-owned business.

Jill is a powerful speaker with the rare ability to deliver substantive content in a way that is engaging and easily accessible. She is also a Professional Member of the National Speakers Association.

Jill resides in Minneapolis, Minnesota.

Talk to Jill about how her Consulting Services can help you gain the clarity you need to develop your business strategies. Book Jill to Speak at your next event. Contact her at:

        www.jcs-usa.com
        www.twitter.com/JillJohnsonUSA
        www.facebook.com/JohnsonConsultingServices
        www.linkedin.com/in/JohnsonConsultingServices

ACKNOWLEDGMENTS

Thank you to everyone who encouraged me to share this book series with the world. You have made this book possible.

To my family:
To my husband, Jack Tebbe. Thank you so much for your endless support of me and for always believing in my dreams.

To my sister, Jaci Johnson. Your insight and feedback have always been extraordinarily valuable to me.

To my book team:
Isabella Dotzler for sharing your editing skills and ideas as I pieced together the detailed concepts for this book series.

Lorelei Kraft for encouraging me to move forward with writing a book.

Kristen Brown for guiding me on making this book series concept tangible.

Maddi Meierotto for your assistance in helping me think through the power of quotes.

Amy Mathews for helping me finally see the possibilities for this book series.

Rachel Benrud for keeping me on track to finally getting this done.

Chris Mendoza for the cover design and formatting to turn my idea into a reality.

To my valued insight team:
To the 5 generations of colleagues and friends who took time out of their busy days to review these books and provide me with valuable feedback to narrow the focus down to the most critical questions. Your responses and comments proved these concepts transcend generational divides.

Bob Baynton, Patty DeDominic, Isabella Dotzler, Mary Frantz, Sharon Gifford, Maddy Gildersleeve, Sharon Horne, Katherine Hunt, Joan Kennedy, Susan McCloskey, Maddi Meierotto, Anne Neu, Kim Utecht Payfrock and Melissa Sauser.

INTRODUCTION

Each day leaders try to bring their best efforts to their work. Yet many are overwhelmed by the complexities of today's constantly changing and unpredictable economic environment. They struggle to find focus to set the strategies they need to lead their enterprises and move their organizations forward.

Our economic, political and social environment is exceptionally volatile, uncertain, complex and ambiguous. As a result, it has become increasingly difficult to develop strategies for success when every time you turn around there is another challenge that threatens your enterprise survival. You have to navigate the challenge of leading a diverse workforce with teams comprised of different generations and widely varied understanding of the strategic roadblocks ahead. To lead in this environment, you need more from yourself and your team.

As a management consultant for more than 20 years, the executives, business owners and board of directors I work with struggle deeply with these issues. In my experience, those leaders who are open to reflection are often the most successful, the most effective, and achieve the greatest results. They are also the most confident in their leadership because they know they have considered every possible aspect of their strategies, opportunities and decisions.

Leaders who are willing to shift their mindset from their current status quo thinking will typically execute business strategies that achieve a higher level of accomplishment. Those who take the time to reflect on their options for responding to evolving market opportunities before they are in chaos have more insight and develop confident strategies to respond and take advantage of unforeseen circumstances. They also find new meaning in their roles and their own potential for business achievement.

Leaders who diligently develop their abilities and continually refine their decision making skills are more effective than their peers. They are more confident in executing strategies and decisions because they have reflected deeply on the available options and understand the consequences of their actions or inaction. They have fully considered their opportunities and are more prepared to adjust their assumptions to the evolving challenges they face.

Leaders who involve their teams in candidly discussing critical issues gain enhanced commitment to achieving enterprise goals and better buy-in when they need them to change. This is because they all understand the stakes and have a clear understanding of the issues they need to address. They are not content to wait to have strategic discussions only at an annual planning meeting. By seeding strategic issues into on-going conversations throughout the year, these leaders know they are not only building the critical thinking skills of their team members, but also providing them with the understanding of the challenges so they can bring their best ideas and innovations forward throughout the year.

Over the years, these insights have evolved into what I use as the framework for my approach to consulting. I call it the BOLD Approach. The BOLD Approach is the foundation of my management consulting practice. Regardless of the setting, this approach has provided my clients with the leadership insights they need to address critical issues threatening their survival and on-going ability to compete. This approach works in the executive suites of corporations, in entrepreneurial environments, in non-profit enterprises and in trade associations.

I have found this is one of the most effective methods you can employ to lead in an unstable business climate. It is a four-point framework to focus your strategic mindset on gaining the insight and critical skills you need to thrive. The Bold Approach is designed to impact your critical situations, influence outcomes and help you achieve greater results.

The components of the BOLD Approach focus on four key areas of review:

- Business Strategies - Grow your organization with purpose and prosperity
- Opportunities - Uncover the maximum potential in your market
- Leadership - Lead with confidence and impact
- Decision Making – Gain clarity to minimize indecision and uncertainty

My clients are success-oriented and ambitious leaders just like you. They share my passion for results and are prepared to act boldly to attain them. They want to understand the critical market forces shaping the future of their enterprises. They seek candor and are not afraid of adapting their strategic thinking to respond to evolving market and competitive dynamics.

Like you, my clients are always searching for insight and information. But knowing the critical questions to ask requires more than desire; it requires a deep focus on asking the right questions. This is why I developed the BOLD Questions Series for you.

GETTING STARTED

Each book in the BOLD Questions Series is designed to guide you through reflection on a key element of the BOLD Approach. They are all carefully constructed to be a tool to guide your thinking and help you better focus on the most critical issues you face.

The BOLD Questions Series is designed to help you obtain the information and insight needed to achieve success. The drive toward success requires diligent action and taking time for reflection.

The quotes and issues you will find in this four volume series reflect the critical issues and key questions I ask my management consulting clients as I help them develop their strategic plans, create their strategies to maximize their growth, or resolve a turn-around situation. By addressing these questions, it will be like having me on-site with you as your personal consultant challenging your thinking and working with you to enhance your strategic mindset. The best way to use this series is to pick one key area you want to focus on and then begin.

Each book in this series hones in on 52 issues and questions you must consider. First you read the quote. Then I ask you to reflect on one or more critical questions relating to the quote. But reflection is not enough. You are then challenged to identify the actions you will take to address the question to resolve the issues or move to the next step toward your success.

Some quotes will resonate with you more deeply than others. For those quotes and questions you initially want to disregard, take a pause. Each topic was chosen because in my experience these are the difficult issues most leaders face.

When you find a question you want to skip over or only answer superficially, it is vital to recognize this is actually an area you need to focus on with even more reflection and thought! If you think you should dismiss it, you must take more time with it. This is a focus area you do not yet have enough insight to understand how important it is to your success.

HOW TO USE THESE BOOKS

There are two different ways you can use the BOLD Questions Series:

On Your Own – You can use these books as a guide for your own reflections on these topic areas. Pick one book in the series as your initial focus area. Each week select a quote to reflect on. Spend at least 15 minutes reviewing the quote and reflecting on the critical question found on the opposite page. Jot down your thoughts, ideas, concerns, next steps, etc. in the space available under the question. Then decide what you are going to do about it. Use the section called Actions I Will Take to summarize what you will accomplish on this issue in the next week.

With Your Team – These books are also ideal for leaders who want to guide their team in a more focused way and begin a dialog about the issues that matter most to future enterprise success. Start by selecting a book in the series for your team to focus on for the next year. On a weekly basis, assign a quote to the group. Have everyone in the group individually work through the quote and question as described above. They should make notes in their own copy of the book. Then guide your team through a focused discussion of the issue and their thoughts about it. Capture all of their ideas on a sheet of paper or on the complimentary "Actions We Will Take Summary Sheet" available on my website, www.jcs-usa.com. Facilitate their discussion as they bring forward different points of view. Identify the top three actions the group comes up with that will most impact your situation. Then designate responsibility for taking action on these items during the next week to individual members of your team. When your group comes back together the following week, begin the meeting with an update on their progress. When you are done with that update, move on to focus your discussion on the next quote. Use a new copy of the "Actions We Will Take Summary Sheet" each week. By the end of the year, you and your team will have engaged in a deep dive into the most critical issues you face. Your team will be accustomed to thinking more strategically, acting as more effective leaders, making better decisions and achieving results designed to create lasting success for your enterprise.

Once you or your team are done with this book, pick up another one of the books found in this BOLD Questions Series and begin again. This will keep your thoughts and discussions moving forward and focused on the issues that really impact your potential for success.

USING THE BOLD QUESTIONS SERIES

By using the entire BOLD Questions Series, you will build success on a viable future that is grounded in a realistic understanding of your situation, not wishful thinking. You will integrate an action plan for uncertainty into every facet of your strategy development.

By engaging in the disciplined focus of consistently asking the right questions to shape your leadership actions, decisions and strategies, you will sharpen the critical thinking skills necessary to thrive in today's complex business climate.

By considering the challenging questions found in all four of these books, you will have a deeper understanding of your current and evolving situation. You will build your confidence because you are developing business strategies to enhance your success. You will uncover the potential in your markets. You will become a more confident and effective leader. You will make better decisions, and so will your team.

Regardless of where you are at today in your own leadership development, by using the BOLD Questions Series you will become more influential, more impactful, and you will think with a more strategic mindset.

Wishing you much success!

Jill J. Johnson, MBA, President & Founder
Johnson Consulting Services

P.S. Share your progress with me. You can reach me via the following:

Email: Jill@jcs-usa.com

Twitter: @JillJohnsonUSA
LinkedIn: www.linkedin.com/in/JohnsonConsultingServices
Facebook: www.facebook.com/JohnsonConsultingServices

For bulk orders, contact my office
for more information at 763-571-3101.

Access your free download of the
"Actions We Will Take Summary Sheet" at:
www.jcs-usa.com/ActionsWeWillTakeSummarySheet

OPPORTUNITIES EDITION

Effective strategic planning in turbulent times requires a deep assessment of your market opportunities. This environment is driven by significant market forces influencing your enterprise success and long-term potential. These market forces affect your business lifecycle and the on-going value of your product or service offerings to your consumers. You must fully understand the impact of the market forces determining your ability to survive and thrive.

Staying close to your target market is crucial to long-term success. But market needs, wants and desires change over time. You must understand how your market is changing and why. To remain feasible, you need to determine what changes are necessary to meet those evolving market needs.

There are nine key market forces affecting most businesses today: shifting demographics, competitive actions, fluid economic conditions, unstable capital markets, governmental interference affecting regulations and reimbursement, technology evolution, workforce skills and capabilities, industry changes as organizations adapt to these forces, and generational shifts.

You have no control over these market forces. Yet you continually have to adapt and adjust strategies to respond to them.

Are you ready to ask the questions to uncover the potential in your market to achieve sales results? Let's begin.

66Clarity means seeing your market opportunities in their entirety to help you identify what needs to be taken advantage of, changed, or adapted.**99**

Jill J. Johnson

What do you need to see more clearly about your situation?

_____

_____

_____

_____

_____

_____

_____

_____

_____

_____

_____

_____

_____

_____

_____

Actions I Will Take:

_____

_____

_____

_____

" Stay close to decision influencers.
They are an invaluable source
of insight on your consumers'
changing needs. **"**

Jill J. Johnson

Who are the decision influencers for your customers and prospects?

Actions I Will Take:

❝Demonstrate a consistency of product and service quality that your clients and colleagues can rely on over time.**❞**

Jill J. Johnson

How can you be more consistent in your quality?

_____

_____

_____

_____

_____

_____

_____

_____

_____

_____

_____

_____

_____

_____

Actions I Will Take:

_____

_____

_____

_____

"Accurate and in-depth market insight must flow into all aspects of your planning efforts.**"**

Jill J. Johnson

What market insight should impact your planning efforts?

_____

_____

_____

_____

_____

_____

_____

_____

_____

_____

_____

_____

_____

_____

Actions I Will Take:

_____

_____

_____

_____

66Understanding the true size
of your target market is fundamental
to knowing if your business
strategies are viable. **99**

Jill J. Johnson

How can you better understand your market potential?

_____

_____

_____

_____

_____

_____

_____

_____

_____

_____

_____

_____

_____

_____

_____

_____

Actions I Will Take:

_____

_____

_____

_____

66Selling in a complex
sales situation requires deep
consumer insight that is matched
to decision triggers and
promotional strategies.**99**

Jill J. Johnson

How can you influence your customers' decision triggers?

_____

_____

_____

_____

_____

_____

_____

_____

_____

_____

_____

_____

_____

_____

Actions I Will Take:

_____

_____

_____

_____

❝People who only reinforce your opinion are not as valuable to decision making as those who challenge you to see things differently.**❞**

Jill J. Johnson

Who can challenge you to look at things differently? How will they do this?

_____

_____

_____

_____

_____

_____

_____

_____

_____

_____

_____

_____

_____

_____

Actions I Will Take:

_____

_____

_____

_____

66Information provides you with
the objective insight you need to
make more effective decisions.**99**

Jill J. Johnson

What objective information do you need for your decisions?

_____

_____

_____

_____

_____

_____

_____

_____

_____

_____

_____

_____

_____

_____

_____

_____

Actions I Will Take:

_____

_____

_____

_____

_____

"One of the most significant factors impacting strategy development is the influence of changing target markets.**"**

Jill J. Johnson

How well does your target market match your business goals?

_____

_____

_____

_____

_____

_____

_____

_____

_____

_____

_____

_____

_____

_____

Actions I Will Take:

_____

_____

_____

_____

"The psychological component
of why your customers buy is the
most critical insight you need to
plan your sales strategy.**"**

Jill J. Johnson

What psychological factors influence your customers?

_____

_____

_____

_____

_____

_____

_____

_____

_____

_____

_____

_____

_____

_____

_____

_____

Actions I Will Take:

_____

_____

_____

_____

_____

"Developing rapport with each sales prospect requires the ability to discover everything you can about their unique situation. It may not be unique to YOU, but it is to them."

Jill J. Johnson

How are you building rapport with your clients?

_____

_____

_____

_____

_____

_____

_____

_____

_____

_____

_____

_____

_____

_____

_____

Actions I Will Take:

_____

_____

_____

_____

"Smart leaders take calculated
risks. They manage the
downside as much as they
do the opportunity. **"**

Jill J. Johnson

What risks do you better need to manage? How will you do this?

_____

_____

_____

_____

_____

_____

_____

_____

_____

_____

_____

_____

_____

_____

Actions I Will Take:

_____

_____

_____

_____

❝You have to be comfortable with the fact that you're going to ask for the sale. Many sales people hesitate and never ask the prospect for the order.❞

Jill J. Johnson

What do you need to ask for in order to get the sale?

_____

_____

_____

_____

_____

_____

_____

_____

_____

_____

_____

_____

_____

_____

_____

_____

Actions I Will Take:

_____

_____

_____

_____

_____

66 *Those who succeed over the long-term are different. They plan for their success. Then they act.* 99

Jill J. Johnson

What do you need to implement to enhance your success?

_____

_____

_____

_____

_____

_____

_____

_____

_____

_____

_____

_____

_____

_____

Actions I Will Take:

_____

_____

_____

_____

66Adjust your communication approach to match your buyer's unique needs and interests. Match your messages to their expressed desires. **99**

Jill J. Johnson

How can you communicate more effectively with your customer?

_____

_____

_____

_____

_____

_____

_____

_____

_____

_____

_____

_____

_____

_____

Actions I Will Take:

_____

_____

_____

_____

66Not everything you try will work ... but that doesn't mean you should stop your efforts.99

Jill J. Johnson

What else can you try to enhance your opportunities for success?

_____

_____

_____

_____

_____

_____

_____

_____

_____

_____

_____

_____

_____

_____

_____

_____

Actions I Will Take:

_____

_____

_____

_____

_____

"Effective planning in turbulent
times requires a deep assessment
of the market forces influencing
your business environment.**"**

Jill J. Johnson

What changing market forces will influence your strategies?

_____

_____

_____

_____

_____

_____

_____

_____

_____

_____

_____

_____

_____

Actions I Will Take:

_____

_____

_____

_____

66 *Understand the decision triggers for your prospects. This will move them more rapidly through the decision continuum to achieve a sale.* 99

Jill J. Johnson

What are the top decision triggers for your prospects?

_____
_____
_____
_____
_____
_____
_____
_____
_____
_____
_____
_____
_____
_____
_____

Actions I Will Take:

_____
_____
_____
_____
_____

"The best advisors are the ones
that challenge your status quo and
challenge your thinking about
your market opportunities.**"**

Jill J. Johnson

Who are the internal and external advisors who challenge your thinking about your opportunities?

_____

_____

_____

_____

_____

_____

_____

_____

_____

_____

_____

_____

_____

Actions I Will Take:

_____

_____

_____

_____

_____

66Take action on your decisions.
It is not enough to just talk
about it. Make it happen! **99**

Jill J. Johnson

What can you do to implement your decision?

_____

_____

_____

_____

_____

_____

_____

_____

_____

_____

_____

_____

_____

_____

_____

_____

_____

Actions I Will Take:

_____

_____

_____

_____

_____

66 *Those who reach too high before their cash, talent, or operational capability are ready for that higher level of success, risk losing everything.* 99

Jill J. Johnson

What do you need to learn to achieve greater success?

_____

_____

_____

_____

_____

_____

_____

_____

_____

_____

_____

_____

_____

_____

Actions I Will Take:

_____

_____

_____

_____

66*If you are listening, your market will tell you where your real business opportunities lay.* **99**

Jill J. Johnson

What is your market telling you about what they want?

_____

_____

_____

_____

_____

_____

_____

_____

_____

_____

_____

_____

_____

_____

_____

_____

Actions I Will Take:

_____

_____

_____

_____

_____

66 The on-going feasibility of
your enterprise is significantly
influenced by the market forces
that impact your business. 99

Jill J. Johnson

What market forces influence your opportunities?

Actions I Will Take:

"By thinking about your clients as identifiable groups, you can develop tactics to move your leads move effectively though their decision continuum."

Jill J. Johnson

What are the key clusters of your customers?

_____

_____

_____

_____

_____

_____

_____

_____

_____

_____

_____

_____

_____

_____

_____

Actions I Will Take:

_____

_____

_____

_____

❝Leverage market intelligence
to identify evolving trends. **❞**

Jill J. Johnson

What market trends should you evaluate further?

_____

_____

_____

_____

_____

_____

_____

_____

_____

_____

_____

_____

_____

_____

_____

_____

Actions I Will Take:

_____

_____

_____

_____

66 *Effective leaders adapt to their evolving market reality.* **99**

Jill J. Johnson

What do you need to adapt to respond to changes in your market?

_____

_____

_____

_____

_____

_____

_____

_____

_____

_____

_____

_____

_____

_____

_____

Actions I Will Take:

_____

_____

_____

_____

"In a complex sale, your prospect
is making many decisions.
They are not just making the
decision to buy you. **"**

Jill J. Johnson

Which decision is your prospect trying to make right now?

_____

_____

_____

_____

_____

_____

_____

_____

_____

_____

_____

_____

Actions I Will Take:

_____

_____

_____

_____

"Look for options. Look for information. Look for insight that will challenge you to think differently about your market.**"**

Jill J. Johnson

Where can you find information and insight to challenge your thinking?

_____

_____

_____

_____

_____

_____

_____

_____

_____

_____

_____

_____

_____

_____

_____

_____

Actions I Will Take:

_____

_____

_____

_____

"Complex demographic shifts
are expected to impact
virtually all industries into the
foreseeable future. **"**

Jill J. Johnson

How will changing demographics impact your opportunities?

_____

_____

_____

_____

_____

_____

_____

_____

_____

_____

_____

_____

_____

_____

_____

Actions I Will Take:

_____

_____

_____

_____

"The declining ratio of working people to retirees will strain social services, pensions & health systems."

Jill J. Johnson

How will population changes impact your future?

_____

_____

_____

_____

_____

_____

_____

_____

_____

_____

_____

_____

_____

_____

Actions I Will Take:

_____

_____

_____

_____

_____

66 The biggest challenge in a sale is
to find ways to determine if your
prospect is really the right client. 99

Jill J. Johnson

How can you decide if your prospect is really the right client for you?

_____

_____

_____

_____

_____

_____

_____

_____

_____

_____

_____

_____

_____

_____

_____

Actions I Will Take:

_____

_____

_____

_____

_____

"Know what customers, product and services lines make money for your company. Start to think like a Chief Financial Officer."

Jill J. Johnson

What makes money for your company?

_____

_____

_____

_____

_____

_____

_____

_____

_____

_____

_____

_____

_____

_____

_____

_____

Actions I Will Take:

_____

_____

_____

_____

"Don't talk about your product or service BEFORE your prospects tell you what is important to them. Probe them to learn what problem they are trying to solve."

Jill J. Johnson

What do you need to reconsider to make your sales conversations more effective?

_____

_____

_____

_____

_____

_____

_____

_____

_____

_____

_____

_____

_____

Actions I Will Take:

_____

_____

_____

_____

"The key to clarity is to see things as they really are, not as you wish them to be.**"**

Jill J. Johnson

What do you need to see and think about more clearly?

_____

_____

_____

_____

_____

_____

_____

_____

_____

_____

_____

_____

_____

_____

_____

_____

Actions I Will Take:

_____

_____

_____

_____

_____

" *Effective sales people understand that a one-size fits all approach is no longer effective.* **"**

Jill J. Johnson

How can you better customize your sales pitch?

_____

_____

_____

_____

_____

_____

_____

_____

_____

_____

_____

_____

_____

_____

Actions I Will Take:

_____

_____

_____

_____

66 There are competing goals in
a sales situation. You want to make
the sale. Your prospects want to
make the right decision. **99**

Jill J. Johnson

How can you balance these competing goals?

_____

_____

_____

_____

_____

_____

_____

_____

_____

_____

_____

_____

_____

_____

_____

Actions I Will Take:

_____

_____

_____

_____

66The more you understand what
drives decision-making for your best
customers, the better you will be able to
focus your marketing messages. **99**

Jill J. Johnson

What drives the decision making of your best customers?

_____

_____

_____

_____

_____

_____

_____

_____

_____

_____

_____

_____

_____

_____

Actions I Will Take:

_____

_____

_____

_____

66Make sure you have the right talent on your team evaluating your market opportunities.**99**

Jill J. Johnson

What skills do you need your team to have now? Do they have them?

_____

_____

_____

_____

_____

_____

_____

_____

_____

_____

_____

_____

_____

_____

_____

_____

Actions I Will Take:

_____

_____

_____

_____

_____

❝Having the right advisors can be key when you are stuck on a critical decision. This is when you most need objective perspective.**❞**

Jill J. Johnson

Who can you reach out to, or hire, to assist with your decision?

_____

_____

_____

_____

_____

_____

_____

_____

_____

_____

_____

_____

_____

_____

Actions I Will Take:

_____

_____

_____

_____

"Help your prospects better understand what you are trying to sell to them. Don't assume they know.**"**

Jill J. Johnson

How is what you sell of real value to your customers?

_____

_____

_____

_____

_____

_____

_____

_____

_____

_____

_____

_____

_____

_____

_____

_____

_____

Actions I Will Take:

_____

_____

_____

_____

66It is difficult to develop effective strategies at the same time you are dealing with significant volatility.**99**

Jill J. Johnson

How is volatility impacting you now?

_____

_____

_____

_____

_____

_____

_____

_____

_____

_____

_____

_____

_____

_____

_____

_____

Actions I Will Take:

_____

_____

_____

_____

"Opportunities abound for
smart marketers to capitalize
on emerging trends.**"**

Jill J. Johnson

What emerging trends should you examine?

_____
_____
_____
_____
_____
_____
_____
_____
_____
_____
_____
_____
_____
_____
_____
_____

Actions I Will Take:

_____
_____
_____
_____

"External market forces determine the future of our businesses. We have little ability to influence most of them. So we must adapt our strategies to leverage them."

Jill J. Johnson

What market forces shape your business future?

_____

_____

_____

_____

_____

_____

_____

_____

_____

_____

_____

_____

_____

_____

_____

_____

Actions I Will Take:

_____

_____

_____

_____

_____

66You can no longer assume
things will remain status quo.
Market forces are constantly
influencing our opportunities.**99**

Jill J. Johnson

What market forces influence your opportunities?

_____

_____

_____

_____

_____

_____

_____

_____

_____

_____

_____

_____

_____

_____

_____

_____

Actions I Will Take:

_____

_____

_____

_____

❝Complex sales do not resolve
in one single interaction. They involve
a series of intricate interactions
and decision points.**❞**

Jill J. Johnson

What customer interactions do you have before a sale?

_____

_____

_____

_____

_____

_____

_____

_____

_____

_____

_____

_____

_____

_____

Actions I Will Take:

_____

_____

_____

_____

66The most effective leaders are
those who acknowledge errors or
market challenges. Then they make
adjustments and move forward. 99

Jill J. Johnson

What issues should you acknowledge and deal with right now?

_____

_____

_____

_____

_____

_____

_____

_____

_____

_____

_____

_____

_____

_____

_____

_____

Actions I Will Take:

_____

_____

_____

_____

_____

66Take action on your ideas. It is
not enough to just talk about it.
Make it happen! **99**

Jill J. Johnson

What action(s) can you take next to put your idea(s) forward?

_____
_____
_____
_____
_____
_____
_____
_____
_____
_____
_____
_____
_____
_____

Actions I Will Take:

_____
_____
_____
_____

66 *The key to target marketing is to focus on the clients you can best serve and who generate your desired profit.* **99**

Jill J. Johnson

How can you better focus on your best clients?

_____

_____

_____

_____

_____

_____

_____

_____

_____

_____

_____

_____

_____

_____

_____

Actions I Will Take:

_____

_____

_____

_____

"Numerous market forces will influence your market opportunities and sales potential.**"**

Jill J. Johnson

What changing market forces will influence your sales strategies?

_____

_____

_____

_____

_____

_____

_____

_____

_____

_____

_____

_____

_____

_____

_____

Actions I Will Take:

_____

_____

_____

_____

66 Match your revenue streams
to what your target market needs,
desires and can realistically afford -
both now and into the future. **99**

Jill J. Johnson

How well does your target market match your business goals?

_____

_____

_____

_____

_____

_____

_____

_____

_____

_____

_____

_____

_____

Actions I Will Take:

_____

_____

_____

_____

66 *The most effective sales people become trusted allies with their customers to resolve their problems.* **99**

Jill J. Johnson

How can you become a trusted "ally" to your prospect?

_____

_____

_____

_____

_____

_____

_____

_____

_____

_____

_____

_____

_____

Actions I Will Take:

_____

_____

_____

_____

❝To achieve success, you
have to be bold!**❞**

Jill J. Johnson

How can you be bolder?

_____

_____

_____

_____

_____

_____

_____

_____

_____

_____

_____

_____

_____

_____

_____

_____

_____

Actions I Will Take:

_____

_____

_____

_____

_____

Also Available in the BOLD Questions Series...

Business Strategy Edition

52 questions to shape your **business strategies.**

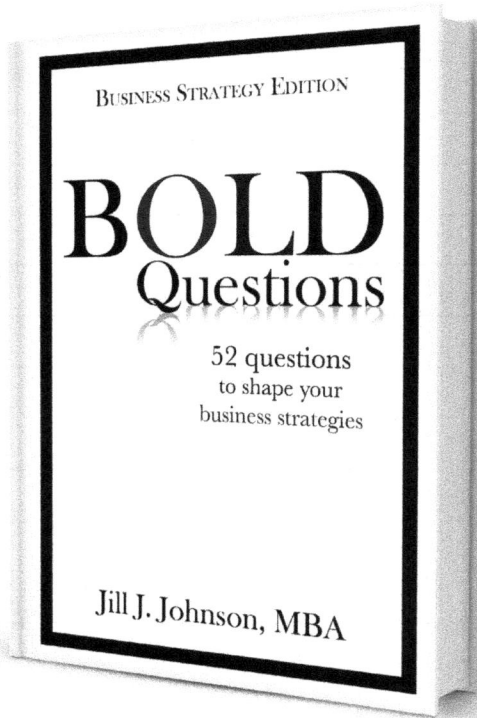

BUSINESS STRATEGY EDITION

BOLD
Questions

52 questions
to shape your
business strategies

Jill J. Johnson, MBA

PURCHASE Your Copy NOW!
Bulk discounts available.

www.jcs-usa.com

Johnson
Consulting
Services
Marketing & Management Consultants

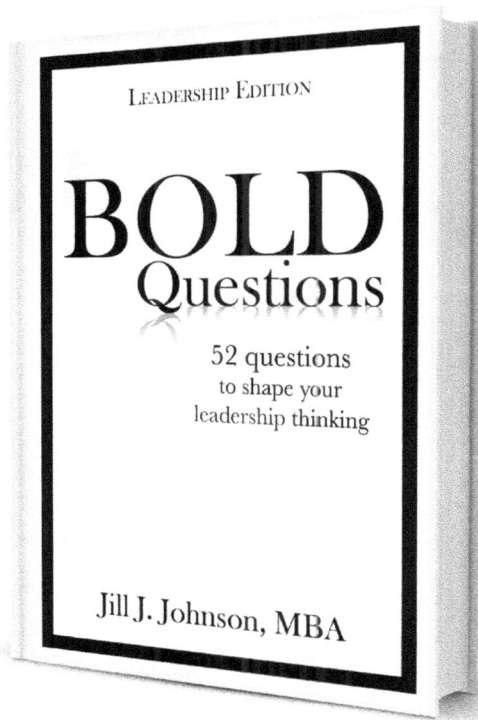

Also Available in the BOLD Questions Series...

Decision-Making Edition

52 questions to shape
how you make **decisions**.

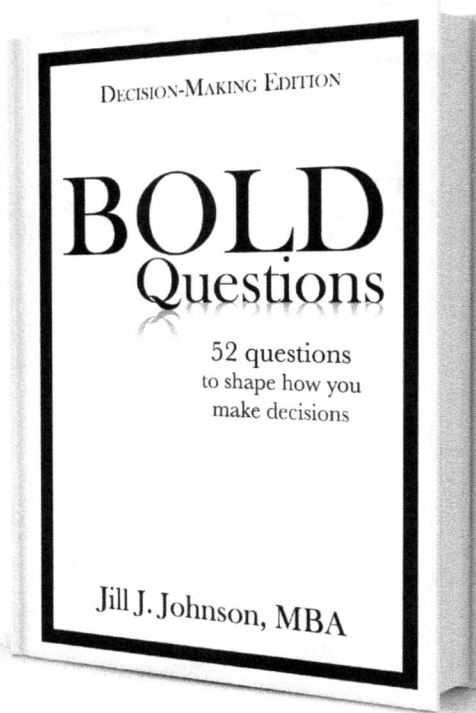

PURCHASE Your Copy NOW!
Bulk discounts available.

www.jcs-usa.com

Johnson
Consulting
Services
Marketing & Management Consultants

Also Available...

Compounding Your Confidence

Transform your future with these
strategies to build your confidence.

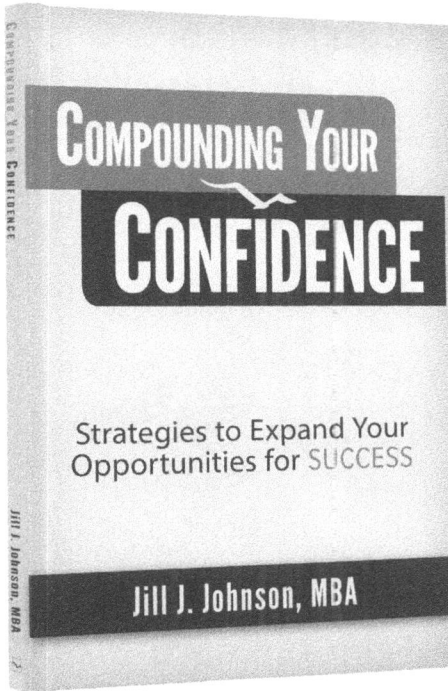

PURCHASE Your Copy NOW!
Bulk discounts available.

www.jcs-usa.com

Johnson
Consulting
Services
Marketing & Management Consultants

www.ingramcontent.com/pod-product-compliance
Lightning Source LLC
Chambersburg PA
CBHW071155200326
41519CB00018B/5239